TECH TRACK™

BUILDING YOUR CAREER IN IT

# BECOMING A
# QUALITY
# ASSURANCE
# ENGINEER

## JASON PORTERFIELD

Rosen
YA™
New York

Published in 2018 by The Rosen Publishing Group, Inc.
29 East 21st Street, New York, NY 10010

Copyright © 2018 by The Rosen Publishing Group, Inc.

First Edition

**Library of Congress Cataloging-in-Publication Data**

Names: Porterfield, Jason, author.
Title: Becoming a quality assurance engineer / Jason Porterfield.
Description: New York : Rosen Publishing, 2018. | Series: Tech track: building your career in IT | Includes bibliographical references and index. | Audience: 7–12.
Identifiers: LCCN 2017001629 | ISBN 9781508175629 (library bound book)
Subjects: LCSH: Quality assurance—Vocational guidance—Juvenile literature. | Quality control—Vocational guidance—Juvenile literature.
Classification: LCC TS156.6 .P67 2017 | DDC 658.5/62023—dc23
LC record available at https://lccn.loc.gov/2017001629

*Manufactured in China*

# CONTENTS

# INTRODUCTION

Software companies are often bustling, as programmers, engineers, and developers work to push through new programs or updates to existing ones. Whether the company is a global business that employs thousands of people or a small start-up with fewer than a dozen employees, one of the busiest departments is likely to be the quality assurance team. They spend their working hours poking and prodding at software in an attempt to find programming errors. If they don't find mistakes, they try different approaches. They may take days or even weeks with the program, using and abusing it in every way imaginable in an attempt to see how it holds up.

The quality assurance engineer is the person who leads these testing efforts. He or she works with the developers to figure out exactly what the software is supposed to do and then proceeds to look for ways to make it crash or act up in some other way. Quality assurance engineers design tests for their teams to run on the software, write programs that probe for vulnerabilities, and establish the scenarios and parameters for tests. The entire time that the testing is under way, they receive feedback from their testers and compile reports. Once the tests are complete, they give reports of their findings to the developers and interpret their findings so that any necessary changes can be made. If changes are made, the quality assurance engineer leads another series of tests until everything is working as well as possible.

This work makes the quality assurance engineer one of the most important specialists in the world of software development. The results of these tests can mean the difference between releasing a successful product that will please the company's customers or releasing a substandard program that is difficult to use and doesn't work as intended. The quality assurance engineer has to develop

*The smartphone boom has created new programming opportunities. The work of a quality assurance engineer may make the difference between a successful app rollout and a flop.*

the best tests possible and get the best results possible out of his or her team. These engineers also have to be able to interpret results and report them in a way that the programmers can understand.

Those are some big responsibilities, and a quality assurance engineer has to receive a proper education in order to become ready for them. Preparation may start as early as elementary school for some, when they first start taking computer classes. On the other hand, their interest may not develop until high school or even college. Either way, a bachelor's degree in computer science is almost always a requirement for

quality assurance engineers. However, many do start out as quality assurance testers, a position that may require only a high school diploma. Two-year college programs and vocational classes can also provide a valuable background education for aspiring quality assurance engineers.

Developing an interest in how computers work at an early age could put someone on the path to becoming a quality assurance engineer even before high school.

The career outlook for quality assurance engineers is strong, as software is playing an increasingly large role in daily life. With the right combination of education, leadership abilities, and communication skills, a determined individual can reach great heights in the field of quality assurance.

# CHAPTER ONE

# THE IT BONANZA

Professionals in the information technology (IT) field work with computers, software, and the infrastructure needed to make certain that everything is working together properly. The growing number of mobile devices and other connected products has greatly expanded the job opportunities for IT workers.

## A CONNECTED WORLD

Information technology refers to the use of any computers, storage devices, networking mechanisms, and digital processes to create, store, process, and share electronic data in many forms. This data can take the form of word processing files, images, complex computer programs, or even games. The IT field includes professionals who design, build, test, operate, and secure information technology.

Information technology has been constantly developing since Charles Babbage (1791–1871) designed the first programmable computing machine in 1822. The first electronic computers were developed during the 1940s and relied on paper punch cards to operate. Those machines weighed tons and took up massive amounts of space. Using these gigantic machines took teams of people who performed specific roles, essentially marking the origins of the IT field.

The earliest computers were extremely expensive. Only government agencies, colleges, and large companies

*Early computers actually had very little processing power when compared to modern PCs or even smartphones, despite being big enough to fill rooms.*

could afford them. That changed with the development of personal computers (PCs) during the 1980s. Suddenly, relatively small and inexpensive computers were available for use by a single person sitting at a desk. Schools and offices could create their own networks and share information electronically. Information technology professionals became necessary for setting up and operating networks and servers, as well as helping people use these new machines. Programmers were needed to write specialized software for these PCs.

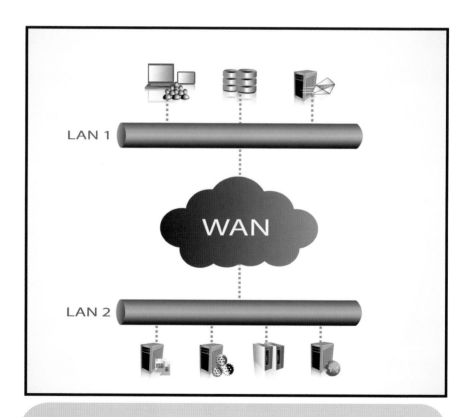

*Programs that are used to share data among a network of PCs must be able to read shared files without creating problems for users.*

The development of local area networks (LANs) and wide area networks (WANs) changed the way in which people interacted with computers. Instead of one person dealing with one computer, many people could share documents and communicate with each other through their PCs. Computers have become much smaller and far more affordable. The development of laptops and smartphones made computer and networking technology portable. Network technology has also made its way into automobiles, home appliances such as smart thermostats, and wearable technology such as fitness bands.

Information technology is used in virtually every field imaginable. Mechanics use computers to diagnose cars, architects use software to design buildings, and doctors can even use smartphones and tablet computers with video capabilities to diagnose patients many miles away. All of these connections bring more people online and put more technology in their hands, broadening the roles for information technology professionals.

Quality assurance engineers are a vital part of that IT world. Depending on their specialty, they test and assess computers, networks, and software. Their role is to make sure that the equipment or programs work smoothly, that the finished product meets the goals of the engineers, and that no new problems have developed.

Specifically, they create the tests that are used to make sure that everything is in working order. They record any problems that come up during the testing process

## Automating the Tests

Many quality assurance tests are now automated. QA profession-als can run scripts—lists of commands that can make software work in a certain way—that replicate the same tasks that they once had to do by themselves. Automated tests allow the testers to work much more quickly and thoroughly. They can even carry out multiple tests at the same time and get more routine tests out of the way while they work on more difficult problems.

While automated testing tools can work faster and more efficiently than human testers, there is little chance that they will ever replace people in QA jobs. In fact, quality assurance profes-sionals perform tests on the automated tools to make sure they do not have any errors. Actual people are much better at judging whether or not a program is easy to use and is performing as well as possible—for now, at least!

*Automated QA testing has not eliminated the need for quality assurance engi-neers. They or their team members still need to be present to make sure the tests are working properly.*

and manage the teams that perform the tests. If problems are found, they communicate their findings to the design engineers, who then go back to correct them. Once the changes have been made, the tests are run again to see if the problems have been fixed.

## ONE HOT MARKET

Information technology professionals are always in demand due to the reliance of businesses on computers and software, as well as the consumer market for products that can be used at home. Job growth in the technology industry has remained steady in recent years, even after factoring in occasional industry bubbles. A Pew Research Center study conducted in 2014 found that the number of core technology jobs—defined as jobs that make technology work for the rest of the population—nearly doubled from 2.2 million in 1997 to approaching 4 million in 2014.

The number of quality assurance engineers has grown in recent years. The job-hunting website Recruiter.com counted 183,110 QA engineers in the United States in 2010. The site predicted that the number would increase to 236,800 by 2018.

Apart from an ever-increasing job market for people with in-demand skills, the tech sector also offers relatively high pay in comparison to other fields. At least 50 percent of the jobs in Glassdoor's 2016 ranking of the twenty-five top-paying jobs in the United States were involved in IT.

Education requirements are not too difficult for pro-spective IT workers to obtain. Some tech jobs may require only a high school diploma; others may call for a two-year associate degree or for the applicant to have earned certification in a particular specialty. More advanced IT jobs require at least a four-year college degree. The tech industry is generally welcoming of people who choose to major in fields other than computer science, as long as they have taken information technology classes and can prove their abilities. More specialized professionals such as quality assurance engineers are often required to obtain at least a relevant bachelor's degree.

IT work also provides a highly stimulating work envi-ronment. Many tasks require problem-solving skills and the ability to think creatively. It helps for IT workers to have a natural curiosity about how programs and hard-ware are designed. In the QA field, this means that they should have an ability to understand the proper use of the software or product and then figure out creative ways to attempt to misuse it. Quality assurance engineers also should have a willingness to test something until it breaks. Instead of simply declaring the product they are testing to be good enough, they have to find inventive ways to check it for vulnerabilities. This requires creative thinking and problem-solving skills.

Companies that produce software or that are involved in web development often have quality assur-ance departments. Quality assurance as a field began in

*Physically damaging a smartphone's screen is one of the most tangible ways a QA engineer can determine whether technology can survive accidents and mishandling.*

factories, where manufactured goods were put through numerous tests to make sure they would hold up under heavy use and misuse. The model shifted to the software industry, where it has become very useful for companies that create programs that must work properly. In this field, programmers often work on only a portion of a project; they may not be able to see where things are not working as well as they should, making it necessary to bring in QA engineers.

# CHAPTER TWO

# INS AND OUTS OF QUALITY ASSURANCE

A quality assurance engineer is responsible for developing the tests that are used to check whether websites and software in development are working properly. They have to study the intended use of the product and understand its intended purpose. They also have to know how to manage a team of testers and how to communicate their findings to the engineers and designers who built the software. Most importantly, they need to be able to assess the performance of the software they are testing and find any flaws that could cause problems in the future.

They may not be interested in what is working correctly. Instead, they look for anything that is not working. They figure out where problems might occur and then find ways to intentionally misuse it to see if it breaks down. They have to be persistent enough to keep trying until they have exhausted every possible problem. Since they bridge the gap between programmers and end users, they must have a solid grasp on what problems a user might have with the program and what the engineers might do to fix these difficulties.

## KNOWING SOFTWARE AND HARDWARE

The work of a QA engineer is often very different from one project to the next, or even from one test to the next. A QA engineer has to examine the software or website itself and may also have to examine the server and other infrastructure pieces. Understanding how software and programming work is absolutely vital to many IT careers. Quality assurance engineers have to understand what the software they are using is supposed to do and how it is supposed to work. This often requires an under-standing of the programming language that was used to build the software.

QA engineers should understand how programming languages translate into machine language. In other words, they need to know how programming languages instruct computers to behave in a certain way.

While QA engineers aren't designing software, they do have to know how to code in order to properly write the scripts that will eventually be used in testing the product. They should know how to write their scripts from scratch if they want to be competitive in the field. Companies often specifically seek out QA professionals who have coding experience. Not having the ability to code puts a QA engineer at risk of not staying up-to-date in the field.

```
148                    this.emit('end');
149                }
150            }))
151            .pipe($.sass({
152                outputStyle: 'expanded'
153            }).on('error', $.sass.logError))
154            .pipe($.autoprefixer(AUTOPREFIXER_BROWSERS))
155            .pipe(isProduction ? $.rename({
156                prefix: 'dt-',
157                suffix: '.min'
158            }) : gutil.noop())
159            .pipe( isProduction ? gulp.dest( paths.styles.buil
160            .pipe( isProduction ? gutil.noop() : browserSync.s
161        });
162
163    // JS
164    gulp.task('js', function() {
165
166
167        var
168
169
170
171
```

*Knowing the programming language that was used to create a program can help the QA engineer spot coding errors that cause problems.*

It helps to know some of the more prominent programming languages and to be familiar with their use. Many QA job listings seek professionals who are able to script well in one or more commonly used coding languages. At the very least, a quality assurance engineer should be skilled in using the language that was used to create the product being tested.

The more commonly used languages include Java, Ruby, and Python. Python and Ruby in particular are known for intuitive coding styles, though both become much more challenging once the programmer moves into more complex operations.

The path to learning a programming language—even a common one—is not always easy. Some QA engineers pick up the basics of the language they need just before testing begins. While this strategy can work, it is better to be prepared well in advance by being experienced in using at least one language, whether in a classroom or workplace setting or simply experimenting with programming at home.

Taking a class in a programming language is an option. In some cases, employers will pay for their quality assurance teams to enroll in a class. The drawback is that many classes—particularly beginning courses—are geared toward programmers who are learning how to write programs. Since QA engineers are more concerned with finding ways to break programs, they have to figure out how to take the programming skills they learn and turn them around in order to find flaws.

Understanding the intentions of the programmers is key when it comes to testing software. Quality assurance engineers should have the communication skills to work with software developers and determine the purpose of the program. Otherwise, it would be hard to tell whether everything is working the way it is intended. Programmers sometimes add extra functions to their products, and they may take away from the program's core purpose.

Communication skills also go the other way. QA engineers need to be able to clearly and tactfully explain any problems they find with the product. If it's not working properly, the developers need to be told so that they can find a solution to the problems. This happens through reports, which should be written as clearly as possible so that the developers know exactly what problems they are fixing and where those trouble spots occur.

Many QA teams also take part in design discussions. In these cases, they know what the development team is planning before the code is written and the test versions created. Experienced quality assurance engineers can often spot bugs or potential problems early in the design process, long before any formal testing is done.

Software developers may be so focused on completing their projects on time that they miss small errors in their code. Catching mistakes early can speed up the development process.

## PROBING FOR FLAWS

Checking software for flaws is often a continuous and evolving process. The programs and applications being tested will likely be in use for years. As time passes, updates will be made and new bugs discovered. Changes will be made to improve functionality. Quality assurance engineers will be involved throughout this work.

The QA agents look for stability issues that may affect the program when it is in use. They look for "bugs"—or stray bits of code—that interfere with the software's ability to work properly. They also look for usability issues, meaning anything that interferes with the average user's ability to run the program correctly. They have to put themselves in the mindset of the consumer and look at the program in the same way that a normal user would.

QA work is complex and collaborative. While each test is different, the testing process itself is not likely to change much from one project to the other. Engineers do not simply poke and prod at the software to see if it works properly. They take the product's intended purpose and create a structured series of tests that will attempt to keep it from working correctly. They run the tests, make note of what happened, and run more tests. They may run the software over and over in order to see if any bugs emerge after repeated use. They try to come up with ways to misuse the product they are testing, whether it is software or a web page. All of this testing happens on a schedule.

Teams may have to fully test a major release as often as once every six weeks. The products they test will likely have multiple features, each of which must be thoroughly checked for flaws. A small feature that may seem insignificant to the design team could make a big difference when it comes to how users interact with the software. A design flaw could be anything from a menu that is difficult to navigate to buttons that don't work in the way the user expects.

QA teams often can't test every aspect of a software release or website launch. They have to prioritize which aspects will be tested most heavily. This is why it is so important to be aware of what the developers are thinking during the design process. When the release in question is an updated version of existing software, the quality assurance engineers may devote the bulk of their time to the areas where the greatest number of changes were made.

Analytical tools such as Google Analytics may be used to figure out which parts of a website or program gets the most use. Feedback from users is also taken into consideration. Bugs in heavily used parts of the program will be prioritized over those in areas that see very little use. However, the bugs that are encountered and reported by users will be addressed before the next release comes out.

The quality assurance team might also divide tasks in order to work more efficiently. Forming teams within the team to look at specific issues such as security and performance can speed the testing process. Aspiring quality assurance engineers may want to consider specializing in

Users who have come to expect software to behave in a certain way would be disappointed if updated versions failed to meet their expectations.

such an area. Doing so can provide added value to one's team and help in the job search process.

## ANALYZING RESULTS

Quality assurance teams stand between the design teams and customers, functioning as a safeguard against releasing faulty products that could damage their company's reputation and even cause real harm to consumers. It is up to them to find bugs before the product is sent out into the market so that these flaws are fixed.

# The Nature of Bugs

Companies invest a lot of time and money to produce software that is free of errors. The QA team is the main line of defense against releasing buggy programs. But what causes bugs to occur in the first place?

Human error is one of the major causes of programming glitches. Software is developed by teams writing thousands of lines of code under pressure. They often work long hours, and even the best programmers sometimes make mistakes. The complexity of the software they are creating can also result in bugs. Every element of the program has to function seamlessly with all others, and programmers might not be able to anticipate potential problems. Third-party tools used to create software can also be buggy, and errors in those programs can result in mistakes being made during the development process. QA teams can provide an additional service by helping programmers find and fix these trouble spots.

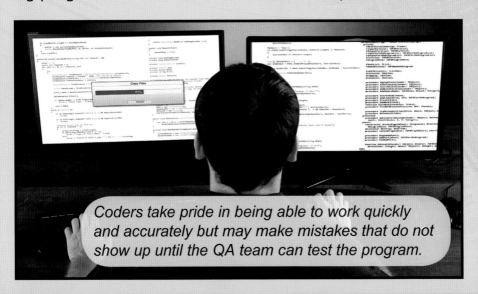

*Coders take pride in being able to work quickly and accurately but may make mistakes that do not show up until the QA team can test the program.*

Throughout the testing process, these engineers are validating that the software is working correctly. They gather the data put out by their tests and analyze it to see where any problems might be occurring. Quality assurance engineers don't fix the problems they find. Instead, the software and the test results are sent back to the development teams. It is up to the developers to make the necessary changes.

The QA team documents the tests that they run, whether they were looking at the larger aspects of the software or smaller parts. Every step taken during testing is recorded so that the developers can see exactly what the testers did to get any negative results. This makes it easier to see exactly where errors occur.

*Taking advantage of hands-on experiments in subjects such as physics can give students a taste of what it's like to test code in a lab setting.*

## A HIGH SCHOOL PATH

High school classes offer more challenges for computer enthusiasts. Middle school computer science classes are geared more toward teaching students that they can have fun and create interesting things with code. In high school, students start to see the real science

Not everyone has a computer. Students who don't have access to computer science classes but are interested in a career in QA should still gain as much experience with computers as possible. If you don't have a computer at home, you should try using a friend's or checking out the computers at school or at your local library. You should also try to learn as much as you can about the operating systems available and how computer hardware and software work.

Students can start learning code as early as they want. Kids in early elementary school are often able to pick up a foreign language more easily than older students. Programming languages are no different. There are many resources available for young students who want to learn on their own, whether they are experimenting with basic logic and building simple programming sentences or creating simple animations and games. For example, Code.org offers students in kindergarten through twelfth grade the opportunity to learn coding through online classes that teach drag-and-drop programming. The Massachusetts Institute of Technology's Scratch program (scratch.mit.edu) also gives learners access to a visual programming language that teaches the basics of building interactive programs such as games and animation.

Schools are placing a greater emphasis on teaching coding in middle school where students often learn the basics of how coding works. Even if they don't learn a specific language, they gain experience through activities such as building games and websites.

## STARTING YOUNG

Many QA engineers begin their career paths in high school or even in middle school, even if they don't know it at the time. These students are drawn to computer science and math classes. They may even spend time learning code on their own. They may also be interested in puzzles and meeting challenges that require outside-the-box thinking, such as locked-room games and technical design competitions. Students who study programming, web development, and engineering will likely leave school with a solid understanding of some of the principles behind quality assurance work.

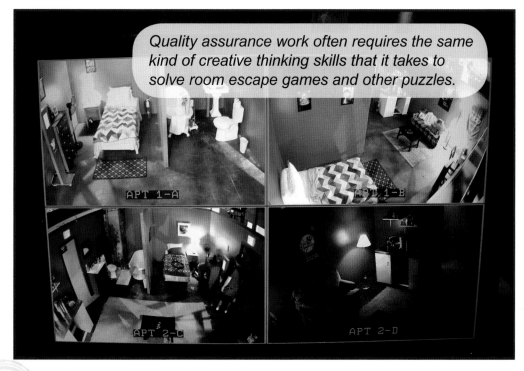

Quality assurance work often requires the same kind of creative thinking skills that it takes to solve room escape games and other puzzles.

# CHAPTER THREE

# An Education in Quality Assurance

Quality assurance engineers have to be knowledgeable regarding the systems for which they are responsible. A college degree helps, though an associate degree or a technical certificate from a vocational program may be enough for QA positions in some fields.

Some companies take an entirely different approach to filling their quality assurance positions. Instead of seeking out employees who have a lot of experience with computer science, they look for people who have the same level of skills as their average customers. While these QA testers may be more likely to think like most consumers in terms of how to use the product, their ability to communicate effectively with the designers and developers may be limited. Building a solid background in computer science is a far safer bet for the student who wants to jumpstart a QA career.

Throughout the testing process, these engineers are validating that the software is working correctly. They gather the data put out by their tests and analyze it to see where any problems might be occurring. Quality assurance engineers don't fix the problems they find. Instead, the software and the test results are sent back to the development teams. It is up to the developers to make the necessary changes.

The QA team documents the tests that they run, whether they were looking at the larger aspects of the software or smaller parts. Every step taken during testing is recorded so that the developers can see exactly what the testers did to get any negative results. This makes it easier to see exactly where errors occur.

# The Nature of Bugs

Companies invest a lot of time and money to produce software that is free of errors. The QA team is the main line of defense against releasing buggy programs. But what causes bugs to occur in the first place?

Human error is one of the major causes of programming glitches. Software is developed by teams writing thousands of lines of code under pressure. They often work long hours, and even the best programmers sometimes make mistakes. The complexity of the software they are creating can also result in bugs. Every element of the program has to function seamlessly with all others, and programmers might not be able to anticipate potential problems. Third-party tools used to create software can also be buggy, and errors in those programs can result in mistakes being made during the development process. QA teams can provide an additional service by helping programmers find and fix these trouble spots.

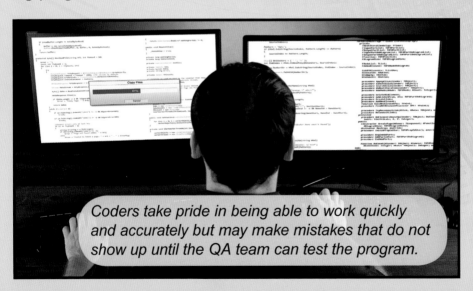

*Coders take pride in being able to work quickly and accurately but may make mistakes that do not show up until the QA team can test the program.*

behind programming; if you're interested, this is the time to explore as many computer science specialties as possible in order to get a feel for the field. Take the general computer science and programming classes that are offered, but also explore any specialized electives such as database management or information assurance and security, if they are available. These options help give an overview of computer science and can help students prepare for the sort of coursework they will encounter in college.

Other high school subjects are also important to succeeding as a QA engineer. Focus on math and science classes. Programmers frequently have to use analytical skills in their work. Gaining a solid grasp of algebra, trigonometry, and plane geometry is essential to sharpening those skills. The majority of computer science programs offered by colleges have numerous math requirements.

Basic science classes are also helpful. Physics in particular deals with similar problem-solving scenarios. Classes that include lab work and group work mirror the sort of collaborative and experimental atmosphere that QA professionals will encounter in the workplace.

English and speech classes can also be important. QA professionals have to be able to effectively communicate with designers and with each other. Knowing how to explain things well in writing or in a presentation given in front of a group of other professionals is vital to doing QA work well. If developers or your fellow team members can't figure out what you're trying to tell them or you are too uncomfortable to put your thoughts in words, it could cause problems.

Students who want to work in quality assurance should take as many computer classes as possible. Focus on learning about how computers work and about the programs and operating systems they use. Exposing yourself to a wide variety of software will provide a solid foundation for learning how programs are supposed to work and finding ways in which they could be improved.

You can also look beyond the classroom for help in charting a path toward a quality assurance career. Read books about testing and become familiar with the terminology used. This will help you get comfortable with QA concepts as you learn about the development cycle and QA's role in it. Students can practice looking for bugs in their own software and writing reports of any flaws they find.

# The STEAM Revolution

Early in the twenty-first century, some people feared that US students were falling behind in science and mathematics, as compared with similar students in other countries. Both subjects are vital for anyone who is interested in engineering and technology. Some schools address this through inclusion of STEAM curriculum, which emphasizes science, technology, engineering, arts and design, and mathematics. These subjects are linked together in an effort to encourage critical thinking while building science and math skills.

STEAM programs are not limited to schools. Some cities and towns also have STEAM programs for students of all ages. These programs may be offered by public libraries, community centers, or even companies. Many of these programs offer instruction in coding, game design, and other computer-oriented areas that could be helpful to students interested in becoming QA engineers.

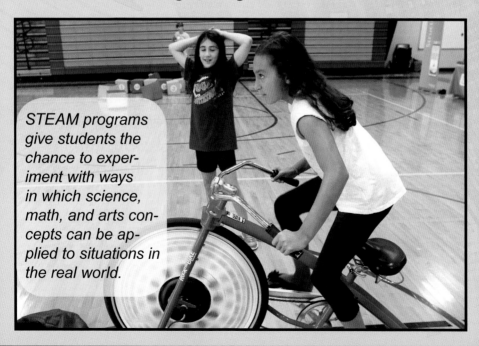

*STEAM programs give students the chance to experiment with ways in which science, math, and arts concepts can be applied to situations in the real world.*

Online discussion groups, computer clubs, and newsletters are good ways to learn some of the ins and outs of the industry. These sources can provide first-hand accounts of what it is like to work in QA and the challenges that these specialists face. They also offer a means of keeping up with new ideas in the industry and changes in technology.

## REACHING A FORK IN THE ROAD

Entry-level quality assurance work sometimes does not require a college degree. Technicians who have taken classes in computer science in high school can usually get jobs as QA testers. Some companies provide training in the specific tests that they run or let their QA workers learn through experience.

However, QA professionals who want to advance to higher positions in the field are usually required to earn a degree. Technical and vocational schools can put students on the path toward earning a two-year degree in computer-related specialties. Earning these degrees may involve taking some classes that seem to have little to do with quality assurance directly. Students may be required to take classes in areas such as network administration, designing and building hardware, and software programming. Ultimately, though, these classes will offer important insight into how software and hardware can be put together—giving aspiring QA professionals the background they need to assess the products they test.

*A strong background in computer science can give you the flexibility you need to work on a wide range of QA projects, including communications and security programs.*

Becoming a full-fledged quality assurance engineer may require earning a four-year degree with a major in a computer-related subject, such as computer science or software design. Quality assurance engineering is still a relatively new field, and as such it is not yet offered as a common major in a four-year college. As a university student, you may find you're instead being asked to learn programming languages and understand networking—in other words, developing the deep understanding of computer science that will help you most in your career. College-level computer science education may also require that you take classes in subjects such as designing hardware, network administration, and microcomputing.

Students who do attend a school that offers a quality assurance concentration within the computer science department will likely have to prove that they have the organizational skills needed to carry out the work. They will have to show that they can plan, put together, and run a quality assurance program. Computer science students usually spend a great deal of time working in computer labs, whether on individual projects or as part of groups. They build and run their own software, checking it for flaws and tweaking it as needed.

## BEYOND THE SCIENCES

Prospective QA engineers will need to prepare themselves with an education that goes beyond work in the computer lab if they are to succeed. In particular, they will need to understand how to be a leader and manage teams of other QA professionals. Learning good communication skills helps, including becoming comfortable with public speaking and giving presentations.

Quality assurance engineers should be comfortable with speaking with engineers, giving instructions, encouraging team members, and both offering and accepting criticism. Being so forthcoming doesn't come easily for many people. Prospective QA professionals can give themselves a boost by taking classes in public speaking or even theater classes. Joining debate clubs and improvisational comedy groups can also help prospective QA engineers become comfortable with speaking in front of others and teach them strategies for overcoming nervousness.

Accounting abilities are also valuable in quality assurance work. Not only do QA engineers need to be able to write code that they can use to test software but they also have to express the software's performance numerically. Numbers help show which parts of the program are living up to expectations and which parts can be improved. Accounting skills help QA professionals show performance speeds, lag times, and other factors in formats that are easy to understand.

Project management and organizational skills are vital to conducting successful quality assurance tests. Testing almost always takes place on a tight deadline. QA engineers must be able to decide which tests need to be run first and which parts of the program are the most important to test. They also should be able to gauge the abilities of their team members and assign tasks based on each person's strengths and weaknesses. QA engineers should be able to set goals and keep the team focused while the tests take place.

## GETTING CERTIFIED

Many industries recognize individuals who have taken the time to learn new skills or become experts in a particular

*QA engineers have to be comfortable speaking in front of people in order to clearly tell their teams about the software they're testing, their goals, and their deadlines.*

area. Professionals who master a certain facet of their industry may earn a license or a certification in that area. A license is a legal document that shows that a person has proven that he or she possesses the knowledge and skills needed to do a certain job and has met certain requirements, such as taking classes or passing exams. Some information technology professionals have to be licensed, depending on where they work and the type of job they have.

Unlike licenses, certifications are not given out by government agencies; they are available through schools and professional organizations. Quality assurance professionals can earn certifications through the Quality Assurance Institute (QAI). QAI provides several official designations that QA workers can earn, including Certified Software Quality Analyst, Certified Manager of Software Testing, Certified Software Tester, Certified Software Project Manager, and Certified Manager of Software Quality.

Earning a certification also demonstrates that the QA professional has taken extra steps to learn about the industry and improve his or her skills. Certifications show that he or she has the skills and the level of expertise needed to carry out certain tasks. Employers look for certifications as a way of seeing whether the individual has put in the time and effort to learn the required skills.

# CHAPTER FOUR

# THE QUALITY ASSURANCE JOB QUEST

Positions as quality assurance engineers are in high demand for qualified individuals. The field remains relatively small when compared to other computer science specialties. However, the impact they have on software development is enormous. QA professionals have the awesome responsibility of detecting any flaws in programs before the public gets the software or sees the website. Their ability to catch bugs before the release of a product can affect whether the launch is a success or a failure.

Prospective quality assurance workers may be able to land a job in their field without a college degree if they can obtain certification. Those who have graduated from a two- or four-year college will have an advantage over those who have not when it comes to competing for QA positions with more responsibility.

## EARLY PREPARATION

Don't let yourself get bogged down too much in the classwork. Computer science students who are interested in a QA career can take their first steps toward finding a job in the field before they are even out of school. Software companies with quality assurance departments sometimes hire promising young workers for summer jobs or even to work on the weekends.

Taking an entry-level QA job provides benefits for both the worker and the company. The worker gains valuable hands-on experience in quality assurance testing and makes connections within the company and the industry—and by starting at the bottom, he or she can learn the basics of the QA industry, common workplace practices, and the company culture. The company benefits by getting the opportunity to check out a potential full-time hire who could easily fill a job opening once he or she graduates.

Entry-level QA positions are often used to perform testing roles. Software testers, for example, actually use the software prototype as a normal user would to make sure that it works properly. They document the bugs that they find and report back to the rest of the team with their findings. In this work, they must be able to carry out the testing plan according to instructions. They must also be knowledgeable enough to spot defects and properly describe these bugs in their reports. Testers also report

*Learning how to code at home can be a good way to familiarize yourself with how programs are designed and where bugs are likely to occur.*

on the usability of the software. They describe parts of the program that worked well and were easy to understand, as well as which parts were harder to use.

Quality assurance testers essentially do their best to make software crash. They may do this by punching keys over and over again or clicking repeatedly on the same button. The work sounds random, but it actually requires great concentration and attention to detail. Testers have to log every move they make. If they do get the program to crash, they have to know the combination of steps they took to make it happen so that they can do it again. Otherwise, the designers and builders won't be able to fix the flaw.

Beginning testers have to know how to use operating systems, databases, spreadsheets, and word processing programs. Depending on what the company does—whether it is in manufacturing, health care, insurance, education, or some other sector of the economy—a working knowledge of that industry can be helpful. If the QA job is with an insurance company, for example, being aware of what the company offers to its customers can be helpful when applying for a job.

College students or recent graduates may want to apply for internships as a way to get acquainted with working in quality assurance. Internships come in many different forms. Some take place during the school year and are part time, often requiring no more than twenty hours of work per week. They may last for a semester or for the entire academic year. Summer internships often last for just three months and require a greater daily time commitment—sometimes a full forty hours. Internships may be paid or unpaid. In the case of unpaid internships, the industry experience gained is considered compensation. Paid internships may offer an hourly or weekly wage or a small stipend to help with living expenses for the course of the internship.

Internships that deal specifically with quality assurance are relatively rare. However, an internship in another position can generate connections that might lead to a job. It never hurts to become familiar with other aspects of the tech industry. Look for internships in areas such

Interns may get to participate in meetings, giving them a first-hand look at how design decisions are made and production schedules are set.

as software development, game design, graphic design, and engineering. The experience gained by sitting in on design meetings, writing code, and learning from professionals can be helpful later when it comes to assessing how well a particular program has been built. Some companies may be more likely to hire a new QA worker who has shown a willingness to learn about specialties outside of his or her chosen field.

## WORKING THE NETWORK

QA professionals land their jobs in several ways. Those lucky enough to have found a QA-related internship may be hired by that company in a full-time role after they graduate. The same could be true for those who worked in an entry-level position while they went to school. Even if those experiences don't lead directly to full-time work, the connections that one makes with other industry professionals can lead to job opportunities at other companies.

Colleges and technical schools often host job fairs and recruiting events throughout the academic year. Computer companies that specialize in designing hardware and software send representatives to the school to meet with interested students. They answer questions about jobs at their firms, describe any open positions, and accept résumés and job applications.

Several companies representing various aspects of the tech industry may be present at a job fair. Recruiting events may consist of a campus visit by representatives of just one company interested in hiring recent graduates. Some business groups and professional organizations hold job fairs in large cities, where tech company representatives can meet with and see résumés from large pools of prospective hires.

Regardless of how big or small a job fair or recruiting event may be, it is important for prospective QA specialists to be presentable and prepared. Recruiters may see hundreds of people at these events, so it is very important to stand out. Prospective employees should dress in businesslike clothing and have updated copies of their résumés ready. They also need to be prepared to talk about their interest in quality assurance and any experience they have in the field. Asking intelligent questions about the company and pertinent job openings there shows an interest in the representative's employers and can help land an interview.

Career fairs are good places to talk to tech company representatives about the products they design and the kinds of applicants they typically hire.

Your university's own computer science department may also prove a good starting point for graduating students entering the job market. Professors often keep in touch with former students, called alumni, who have gone on to work within their fields; in the case of computer

Tech companies such as Minecraft owner Microsoft may offer special tutorial programs designed to help students learn coding and see what the company does on a daily basis.

science professors, this may include connections with current quality assurance engineers. These former students may be willing to talk to promising job-seekers about openings at their companies. Fellow students or former classmates who have already landed positions can also be good sources of information about job openings.

There are a number of large software-oriented and web-related companies that frequently recruit recent graduates for entry-level positions. Microsoft, Google, the computer game company Electronic Arts, and other firms have very active quality assurance departments. These firms often take part in recruiting events or hold their own, inviting potential employees to introduce themselves and explain why they would be a good hire. Larger companies such as these can provide stability and give their new employees room to increase their skills and advance within the company. The pay and benefits offered are usually competitive within the field. Departments may have a well-defined management structure and the resources they need to do their work correctly.

There are some disadvantages to working for one of the larger firms. While they may give their new employees room to grow and realize their potential, they may also offer less career guidance than smaller companies. Management styles may also be less personal. Larger companies may experience a high rate of turnover, as employees leave and new hires come on board. Because they are constantly recruiting, these companies may see

# The Job Interview Puzzle

Job interviews can be stressful and draining. The person being interviewed has to show that he or she is knowledge-able and has the personality and background needed to successfully fill the role, while making a good impression. For QA engineers, part of the interview might involve suc-cessfully solving a logic puzzle. Such puzzles have become increasingly popular at software companies as a way to test whether QA applicants have the creative thinking skills needed to thoroughly test products. Tests may be timed, and there might not even be a single right answer. The testers simply want to see the engineer's thought process at work and how many approaches he or she takes in trying to solve the puzzle. If a successful solution is found quickly, then the interviewee may have an advantage over other applicants.

*Logic puzzles let interviewers see how an applicant thinks. They can also be an oppor-tunity for the job seeker to show how well he or she handles pressure.*

their new hires as being easily replaceable. Larger companies may also experience occasional downturns, during which they make less money and have to adjust by laying off workers. New hires who know the least about how their departments work may be among the first to lose their jobs under these circumstances.

Smaller firms and start-ups may have smaller QA departments, but they also have a desire to find the best employees to fill those roles. A new release plagued by a lot of bugs could sink a small software company, whereas a larger firm might be able to minimize the damage. Smaller firms might not have an organizational structure with such highly defined roles as the larger companies. In start-ups, an employee might be responsible for many tasks that fall outside his or her area of specialty. Salaries and benefits also may be lower and working hours longer because there are fewer employees to help with running the QA tests.

However, employees at smaller companies may be more tightly knit because there are more opportunities for everyone to get to know each other. And smaller salaries may be offset by other benefits, such as shares in the company. Some of the appeal of start-ups, one could argue, is the excitement of being part of something new that has the *potential* to become a major success.

# THE WORKING ENVIRONMENT

Testers try to use the software—and misuse it—in every possible way, according to the test plan developed by the QA engineers. This means that they spend several hours per day using the same program. If they work for a video game company, for example, they may spend their entire workday playing the same game over and over. For this reason, QA work can get boring at times. Even a fun, well-designed game will likely get old after playing it for hours over the course of days or weeks. This is especially true when playing a game with the goal of finding errors rather than winning.

Even if the process of testing for bugs can get dull, finding one can be thrilling. Maybe it's a minor problem that occurs only rarely and alters the formatting, or it could be a major mistake that causes the program to crash frequently. Regardless of the size of the mistake, every move made before finding it must be logged in detail so that it can be found again. This aspect of QA can be very stressful. A tester has no way of knowing when he or she will come across a bug. When it does happen, he or she has to be able to remember exactly what keystrokes or mouse clicks led up to it and then describe them clearly. QA engineers must be able to concentrate intently on what they are doing in order to log their steps accurately. Even if the tests are automated, the testers have to focus on the monitors so that they know the tests are working properly and to flag points where errors are detected.

Testers and QA engineers communicate frequently. Engineers have to be ready to answer any questions the testers might have about the testing processes, as well as address any concerns raised about whether the tests are performing properly and about whether the testing environment is adequately equipped for the tests being run.

During the time that the tests are being run, the engineers and their teams do everything they can to stay on schedule and ensure that they don't compromise the quality of the tests. They communicate with various developers and departments involved to keep every part of the testing process moving along smoothly. Typically, QA work consists of a forty-hour week. However, as testing deadlines approach, teams may work overtime to fit in as much testing as possible. This is particularly true if the testing starts later than expected, the deadline moves up, or if the testing team encounters serious problems with the software or with the tests that have been devised for it.

As with most careers, there are drawbacks to working in quality assurance. QA engineers and testers spend many long hours sitting and working with the same program over and over. The sameness gets dull. They also have to stare at computer monitors for the greatest portion of their workday, which can cause eye strain and headaches. In addition, QA jobs can be very solitary. Team members will likely spend many days focused on the tests they run and finding flaws. The communication that takes place may be exclusively by instant messaging.

However, the work is often quite rewarding. QA jobs are challenging, and it can be thrilling to meet or exceed the goals of each testing project. It's also a great field for people who are extremely detail oriented and who like to solve problems, such as replicating the steps taken before discovering an error. As a bonus, the ability to painstakingly go through a software program and detect errors is remarkable and can get one noticed. Even though much of the actual testing work is solitary, testing groups can bond quickly while working on a project. While the QA group itself offers opportunities to make friendships and business relationships that can last for many years, the same is also true of other employees you will meet around the company, in common spaces and in sharing mutual goals—such as within the design and development departments.

# CHAPTER FIVE

# THE QUALITY ASSURANCE OUTLOOK

The continued development of new apps and programs—including games, operating system software, file-sharing apps, and security software—guarantees that quality assurance engineers will continue to be in demand, at least for the foreseeable future. While some QA tasks can and have been automated, QA engineers are necessary to develop the tests, make sure they are running properly, and interpret their results.

Typically, the career arc of quality assurance professionals begins at the entry-level position of quality assurance testers. After staying with the company for a while and gaining more experience, they may be promoted to the position of quality assurance analyst. QA analysts bridge the gap between the testers and the QA engineers who oversee the test projects. QA analysts work on test development and perform tests. They also write and update the standards and specifications for the tests used.

QA engineers may look for input from their team members when devising their testing plans, especially ideas about how the product being tested might be misused.

## ON THE JOB

Quality assurance engineers tend to work in comfortable settings, regardless of the size of the company that employs them. They work in offices or in computer labs, depending on how the company is set up. Testing is a complex and time-consuming process, and so it is important that the testers have a comfortable environment in which to run their tests, as well as the computer resources necessary to do the job as thoroughly as time allows.

QA engineers spend their days developing and running tests. The first step is to develop a "test plan," which describes the goals and focus of the testing project, as well as the approach that the testers will take. The plan should include an overview of the product, the goals of the testing effort, assumptions about the software, a description of the tests, the team's priorities and goals, and any limitations placed on testing. The testing environment should be described, as should the metrics used to measure performance.

In developing the test plan, QA engineers think about the software, what it is supposed to do, who is going to use it, and how it is going to be used. If the product is an updated version of the software, they consider the changes that have been made to the existing product and how those changes might affect the functionality of the parts that have not been changed. The test plan helps the designers and developers understand the testing process from start to finish. It allows them to visualize the initial assumptions the test team made regarding how the program should work and the ideas they had for testing its functionality based on those assumptions. The test plan also gives the QA team the opportunity to think about what it would take for them to consider the software products acceptable and ready for release.

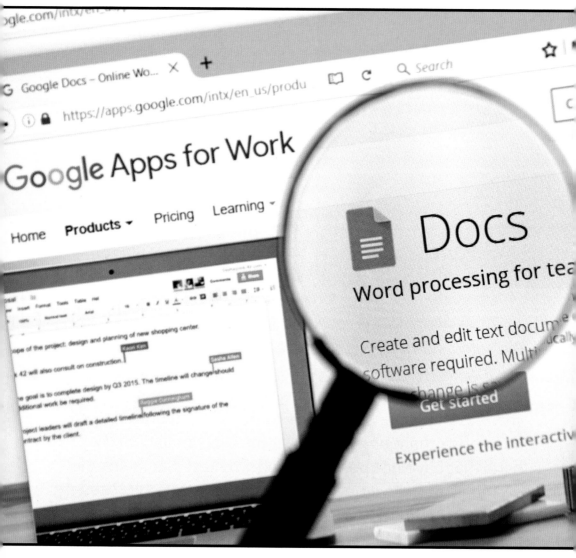

Developing the tests to be used also requires numerous steps. The QA engineers have to hear from software users and the developers to get a picture of the computer program's requirements, internal design specifications, and external design functions. Based on that information and the setting in which the software will primarily be used, they set the testing priorities and identify the parts of the program that will require the most attention from the testers. They figure out the test environment requirements, including the hardware and software they need, as well as any communications tools that might be necessary.

Quality assurance engineers also have to decide what specialized testing software they need, such as automation tools, test tracking programs, analysis tools, and programs for keeping track of bugs. They decide what the labor requirements will be, assign specific tasks to members of their

*Collaboration software suites such as those offered by Google are designed to handle edits from multiple users at once, creating unique challenges for QA engineers.*

team, and put together a timetable describing when they expect to reach important milestones and an estimated completion date.

The process of setting up for a test also includes putting together test scenarios and approaches, as well as preparing the test plan documents. Assembling user manuals, installation guides, reference documents, configuration guides, and any other instructions or resources that an ordinary user would receive with the software is also necessary for replicating how an ordinary user would approach installing and setting up the program. The test tracking processes and the processes for logging and saving testing information will also be set up. Testing scenarios may also have to be written in order to give the testers guidance regarding how to proceed with the tests.

Once the tests are performed, the results are evaluated and reported back to the designers and developers. The bugs that were discovered are tracked down using the testing logs and any necessary repairs are made. The elements of the program that were repaired will be tested again, and the rest of the software may also be tested to make sure that the changes did not alter the functionality of the rest of the program. Once the product is determined to be ready for release into the market, the QA engineer becomes responsible for maintaining the test plans, the testing environment, and the programs used in testing so that the program can be tested again as updates and new versions are developed.

## AREAS OF GROWTH

Information technology is expanding in ways that would have been unimaginable just ten years ago. Recent innovations have changed the way in which software is used and shared. Cloud computing has opened up new horizons. Cloud computing refers to a digital environment in which resources such as storage capacity, data, memory, and software are shared between multiple devices.

The ability to share programs and documents with ease has led to a greater emphasis on designing software with collaboration in mind. For example, traditional word processing programs often allow only one user to make changes at a time. Cloud-based programs such as Google Docs allow multiple users to work simultaneously. Quality assurance engineers have to make sure that the program not only functions as a word processing document should but that it also enables that collaborative work without crashing or creating other problems.

Cloud computing has also enabled the use of powerful mobile devices as the primary means of interacting with software for some people. The rise of smartphones, tablets, and other mobile devices led to a boom in the development of software to meet the demands of those consumers. Apps for those devices are heavily dependent on touch-screen technology that requires precise controls. QA professionals test the ability of the apps to function on a variety of devices, using the same kind of "test it until it breaks" strategies that they would apply to software on a desktop or laptop computer. They test mobile games, media players, social media apps, mapping software, and a variety of other ingenious mobile applications.

Business management software—programs that help businesses keep track of important transactions, expenses, communications, and other important documents—has been around in one form or another for decades. However, these programs have become much more powerful and collaborative in recent years and require rigorous QA testing to assure that those elements function correctly.

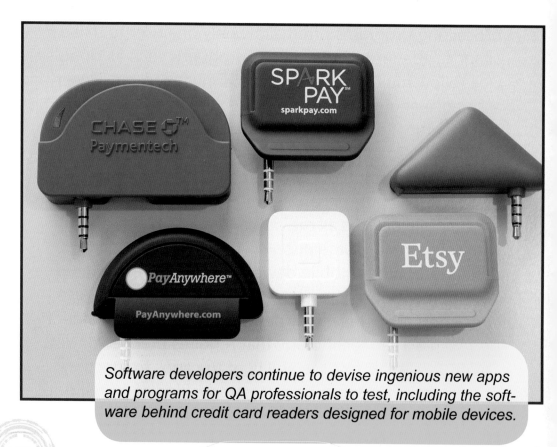

*Software developers continue to devise ingenious new apps and programs for QA professionals to test, including the software behind credit card readers designed for mobile devices.*

Mobile payment systems have become focal points for developers as more people use their smartphones to pay in stores and in restaurants. The payment software has to function properly in order to correctly charge the user's accounts. It also has to be easy to use at both ends—the person making the payment and the person processing it should have no trouble using the payment app at checkout.

## Understanding Cloud Computing

Traditionally, software, documents, and files have been stored on and accessed on a computer, a hard drive, or on a storage device such as a flash drive or disk. In cloud computing, files and programs are stored on networks of servers and accessed through the internet. The data and services are actually stored on multiple servers that must be in communication with each other to deliver what the user needs. Users can access them through a web browser or an app. The cloud frees users from having to go to a specific location or use a specific device to access the files they need. Instead, users can get to the cloud through any internet-enabled device with the right software. Cloud usage is expected to grow in the coming years, meaning that the programs and apps designed for the cloud will also increase.

# JOB SECURITY

Quality assurance engineers are valued members of the workforce at information technology companies. By making sure that the company puts out the best products possible, they can help it increase its business and avoid costly mistakes. Their knowledge of the development process and the techniques they develop for testing products make them indispensable. They manage their teams, communicate openly and effectively with the software developers, and compile the reports that will indicate whether a product is ready for the market or if it needs more fine-tuning.

There is a high demand for QA engineers on the job market. Because they have taken the time and made the effort to advance to that title, they are often seen as having much greater levels of expertise than testers or QA analysts. If they have proven themselves in that role for one employer, it is highly likely that they will be able to land another job in the same position.

QA engineers who manage to find work with an established employer can generally expect a fairly stable work environment. A company such as Microsoft or Apple that has been designing software for decades isn't likely to suddenly go through a round of drastic layoffs unless the company's outlook begins to look really rocky. The wide variety of software products, websites, and apps being developed at any given time means that demand for QA engineers capable of devising and running tests for them will remain strong.

## WHERE TO WORK

The internet has made telecommuting a possibility for people in multiple professions. Workers who live in areas far from where their companies are based can still do their jobs from home, just as if they were actually coming in to the office every day. Some information technology positions are like that, as well. However, quality assurance jobs in general are nearly always on-site. The testing environment and all of the tools the QA team needs are nearly always going to be located in a centralized lab or office.

Quality assurance teams often divide their work between members so that everyone is working on a different part of the program at the same time.

Depending on the size of the company, the testing facilities could be spacious, or they might occupy one corner of a start-up's office. They are likely to be located in or near major technology hubs, where IT companies have a strong foothold. Places like California's Silicon Valley; Seattle, Washington; Chicago, Illinois; and Austin, Texas, are all good places to look. QA jobs might also be available in towns that are home to universities and research facilities that do a lot of IT research and development work. Many start-ups begin on college campuses, opening up the possibility of finding QA engineering work in such a setting. Some IT companies also have offices or facilities in or near college towns, giving them access to bright recent graduates ready to make a good first impression in the quality assurance field.

# GLOSSARY

**APPLICATION**  A piece of computer software designed to do a particular job.

**AUTOMATION**  A system for controlling a process automatically, as by a computer program.

**BROWSER**  A computer program that allows users to search for information and view websites on the internet.

**CERTIFICATION**  Proof that a person possesses certain skills or qualities.

**COLLABORATIVE**  Involving a group of people working together to meet a certain goal.

**COMPUTER SCIENCE**  The branch of engineering that deals with computer hardware and software.

**CRITICAL THINKING**  Carefully analyzing information from many angles in order to make a decision.

**DATA**  Information that can be transmitted or processed by digital means.

**DATABASE**  A structured collection of data that is stored on a computer.

**FACET**  One side of something that has many sides.

**FUNCTIONALITY** The range of tasks that a program can perform for a user.

**INDISPENSABLE**  Something or someone that is absolutely needed.

**MEDIA**  The means of communication, such as radio,

television, and newspapers, that reach or influence people widely.

PROGRAM  A series of instructions that makes a computer perform a certain task or action.

SERVER  A computer that controls or performs certain tasks for other computers in a network.

SMARTPHONE  A mobile phone that also works as a small computer, allowing users to run programs and store data.

SOFTWARE  Programs used by computers for doing certain jobs.

TECHNICIAN  A person who is skilled in the practical use of science or technology.

TELECOMMUTE  To work from outside the office by using telephones, the internet, and email to communicate.

TRANSACTION  The act of buying or selling something or making a business deal.

# FOR MORE INFORMATION

**Canada's Association of IT Professionals**
National Office
60 Bristol Road East
Unit 8 - Suite #324
Mississauga, ON L4Z 3K8
Canada
(905) 602-1370
Website: http://www.cips.ca
CIPS is an organization dedicated to setting standards and establishing best practices for Canada's information technology professionals.

**Computer History Museum**
1401 North Shoreline Boulevard
Mountain View, CA 94043
(650) 810-1010
Website: http://www.computerhistory.org
The mission of the Computer History Museum is to preserve and present for posterity the artifacts and stories of the information age.

**Computer Science Online**
Abuv Media
50 Washington St
#302
Reno, NV 89503
(916) 990 4526
Website: http://www.computerscienceonline.org/
Computer Science Online offers coding assistance,

information about particular computer science disciplines, and information about college programs.

## CS Unplugged

Department of Computer Science and Software Engineering
College of Engineering, University of Canterbury
Private Bag 4800
Christchurch 8140
New Zealand
+64 3 364 2987, Ext: 7727
email: Tim.Bell@canterbury.ac.nz
Website: http://csunplugged.org/
CS Unplugged provides online tutorials, videos, and activities designed to encourage students of all ages to learn coding.

## Hour of Code

c/o Code.org
1501 4th Ave, Suite 900
Seattle WA 98101
Website: https://csedweek.org/
Hour of Code is a program held during Computer Science Education Week, during which people from around the world can learn how to start coding.

## Internet Society

1775 Wiehle Avenue, Suite 201
Reston, VA 20190-5108
(703) 439-2120

Website: http://www.internetsociety.org
This organization works to address issues relating to the
internet, including internet education, standards, and policy.

**MediaSmarts**
205 Catherine Street, Suite 100
Ottawa, ON K2P 1C3
Canada
(613) 224-7721
Website: http://www.mediasmarts.ca
The website for this network contains a selection of digital
literacy resources for students, teachers, and parents.

**National Science Foundation**
4201 Wilson Boulevard
Arlington, VA 22230
(703) 292-5111
Website: http://www.nsf.gov/
The NSF is a government agency that funds scientific
research in a variety of fields.

# WEBSITES

Because of the changing nature of internet links, Rosen
Publishing has developed an online list of websites related
to the subject of this book. This site is updated regularly.
Please use this link to access the list:

http://www.rosenlinks.com/TECHT/quality

Bedell, Jane (J.M.). *So, You Want to be a Coder?: The Ultimate Guide to a Career in Programming, Video Game Creation, Robotics, and More!* (Be What You Want). New York: Aladdin/Beyond Words, 2016.

Foege, Alec. *The Tinkerers: The Amateurs, DIYers, and Inventors Who Make America Great.* New York: Basic Books, 2013.

Freedman, Jeri. *Careers in Computer Science and Programming* (Careers in Computer Technology). New York: Rosen Classroom, 2011.

Furgang, Kathy. *Money-Making Opportunities for Teens Who Are Computer Savvy.* New York: Rosen Publishing, 2014.

Goldsmith, Mike. *Computer.* New York: DK Publishing, 2011.

Henderson, Harry. *The Digital Age.* San Diego, CA: ReferencePoint Books, 2013.

Marji, Majed. *Learn to Program with Scratch: A Visual Introduction to Programming With Art, Science, Math and Games.* San Francisco, CA: No Starch Press, 2014.

Matthes, Eric. *Python Crash Course: A Hands-On, Project-Based Introduction to Programming.* San Francisco, CA: No Starch Press, 2015.

Padua, Sydney. *The Thrilling Adventures of Lovelace and Babbage: The (Mostly) True Story of the First Computer.* New York: Pantheon Books, 2015.

Richardson, Craig. *Learn to Program with Minecraft: Transform Your World with the Power of Python.* San Francisco, CA: No Starch Press, 2015.

# BIBLIOGRAPHY

Alpern, Naomi J., Alpern, Joey, and Muller, Randy. *IT Career JumpStart: An Introduction to PC Hardware, Software, and Networking.* Hoboken, NJ: Sybex, 2012.

Ben-Yehuda, Itay. "Agile QA: Don't Relegate Software Bugs to User Stories." *TechBeacon.* Retrieved October 26, 2016. http://techbeacon.com/agile-qa-dont-relegate-software-bugs-user-stories.

Chemuturi, Murali. *Mastering Software Quality Assurance: Best Practices, Tools, and Techniques for Software Developers.* Plantation, FL: J. Ross Publishing, 2010.

Cohen, Andrew. "Should You Hire a Software Development Intern at Your Startup?" *Entrepreneur.* November 11, 2015. https://www.entrepreneur.com/article/252589.

Desilver, Drew. "How US Tech-Sector Jobs Have Grown, Changed in 15 Years." *Pew Research Center,* March 12, 2014. http://www.pewresearch.org/fact-tank/2014/03/12/how-u-s-tech-sector-jobs-have-grown-changed-in-15-years.

Enelow, Wendy S., and Kursmark, Louise M. *Expert Résumés for Computer and Web Jobs.* Indianapolis, IN: JIST Publishing, 2011.

Fanadka, Karim. "Ten Best Practices for QA Teams to Deliver Quality Software, Fast." *TechBeacon.* Retrieved October 25, 2016. http://techbeacon.com/10-best-practices-qa-teams-deliver-quality-software-fast.

Goldberg, Daniel and Larsson, Linus. "The Unlikely Story of Microsoft's Surprise Minecraft Buyout." *Wired.* June 2,

2015. https://www.wired.com/2015/06
/minecraft-book-excerpt.

King, Julia. "The Evolution of IT Jobs." *CIO*, February 8,
2008. http://www.cio.com/article/2437128/it
-organization/the-evolution-of-it-jobs.html.

Lent, Jennifer. "QA Skills Gap: Testing Pros Need Enough
to Write a Test Script." *TechTarget*. Retrieved October
15, 2016. http://searchsoftwarequality.techtarget.com
/feature/QA-skills-gap-Testing-pros-need-enough-to
-write-a-test-script.

Luck, Marissa. "Seattle's Tech Boom Isn't Just for Rich
Kids: Three Programs Reinvigorating STEM Education."
*Crosscut*. June 11, 2014. http://crosscut.com/2014/06
/seattles-tech-boom-shouldnt-just-be-rich-kids-3-pr.

McLaughlin, Emily. "Information Technology Skills Gap
Raises Concerns for Some." *TechTarget*. June 6, 2014.
http://searchcio.techtarget.com/news/2240222158
/Information-technology-skills-gap-raise
-concerns-for-some.

Naik, Kshirasagar, and Tripathy, Priyadarshi. *Software Testing and Quality Assurance: Theory and Practice*. Hoboken, NJ: John Wiley & Sons, 2011.

Pearce, Rohan. "A Wakeup Call for Software QA." *Comput-
erworld*. October 14, 2013. http://www.computerworld
.com.au/article/528992/wakeup_call_software_qa/.

Poushter, Jacob. "Smartphone Ownership and Internet Usage Continues to Climb in Emerging Economies." *Pew
Research Center*. February 22, 2016. http://www

.pewglobal.org/2016/02/22/smartphone-ownership
-and-internet-usage-continues-to-climb-in
-emerging-economies/

Press, Gil. "A Very Short History of Information Technology (IT)." *Forbes.* April 8, 2013. http://www.forbes.com
/sites/gilpress/2013/04/08/a-very-short-history-of
-information-technology-it/#301db2b570a5.

Shell, Shawn. "Modernizing Business Collaboration Software From the Inside Out." *TechTarget.* September,
2014. http://searchcontentmanagement.techtarget
.com/feature/Modernizing-business-collaboration
-software-from-the-inside-out.

Silverthorne, Valerie. "Facing the Future of Software Testing One Change at a Time." *TechTarget.* Retrieved October 26, 2016. http://searchsoftwarequality.techtarget
.com/feature/Facing-the-future-of-software-testing
-one-change-at-a-time.

Walters, E. Garrison. *The Essential Guide to Computing:
The Story of Information Technology.* Upper Saddle
River, NJ: Prentice Hall, 2000.

Whittaker, James A. *How to Break Software: A Practical Guide
to Testing.* Upper Saddle River, NJ: Pearson, 2002.

# INDEX

representatives (company), 45-46
Ruby, 18

## S

Scratch (program), 29
scripts, 12, 17-18
server, 11, 61
software, 17-20
software developers, 19, 64
software flaws, 21-24
software testers, 41-43, 52-53
stability issues, 21
start-ups, 51, 66
STEAM, 33

## T

technician, 34-35
telecommuting, 65
testing process, 21, 23
test plan, 41-42, 52, 57-58, 60
test scenarios, 31-32, 60

## U

usability issues, 21
user manuals, 60

## W

wide area networks (WANs), 11
work environment, 32, 52-54

# About the Author

Jason Porterfield is a writer and journalist living in Chicago, Illinois. He has written about tech subjects for several publications. Some of his technology books include *Julian Assange and WikiLeaks*, *Tim Berners-Lee*, *White and Black Hat Hackers*, *Careers as a Cyberterrorism Expert*, and *Conducting Basic and Advanced Searches*.

## Photo Credits